GOAL SETTING:

The Ultimate Guide For Side Hustlers

Copyright 2019 by For Side Hustlers

All rights reserved.

This content is provided with the sole purpose of providing relevant information on a specific topic for which every reasonable effort has been made to ensure that it is both accurate and reasonable. Nevertheless, by purchasing this content you consent to the fact that the author, as well as the publisher, are in no way experts on the topics contained herein, regardless of any claims as such that may be made within. As such, any suggestions or recommendations that are made within are done so purely for entertainment value. It is recommended that you always consult a professional prior to undertaking any of the advice or techniques discussed within.

This is a legally binding declaration that is considered both valid and fair by both the Committee of Publishers Association and the American Bar Association and should be considered as legally binding within the United States.

The reproduction, transmission, and duplication of any of the content found herein, including any specific or extended information will be done as an illegal act regardless of the end form the information ultimately takes. This includes copied versions of the work physical, digital and audio unless express consent of the Publisher is provided beforehand. Any additional rights reserved.

Furthermore, the information that can be found within the pages described forthwith shall be considered both accurate and truthful when it comes to the recounting of facts. As such, any use, correct or incorrect, of the provided information will render the Publisher free of responsibility as to the actions taken outside of their direct purview. Regardless, there are zero scenarios where the original author or the Publisher can be deemed liable in any fashion for any damages or hardships that may result from any of the information discussed herein.

Additionally, the information in the following pages is intended only for informational purposes and should thus be thought of as universal. As befitting its nature, it is presented without assurance regarding its prolonged validity or interim quality. Trademarks that are mentioned are done without written consent and can in no way be considered an endorsement from the trademark holder.

Table of Contents

Introduction 6

PART I: Establishing Your Parameters 8

CHAPTER 1: Passion and Possibilities: SMART Goals 11

CHAPTER 2: Programs and Apps: Tools for Success 16

CHAPTER 3: Limits and Learning: Keeping Balance 22

PART II: Achieving Financial Goals 27

CHAPTER 4: Determining Your Future: What Do You Need 30

CHAPTER 5: New Avenues to Success: The Side Hustle 35

CHAPTER 6: Marketing and the Side Hustle: Specific Targets 42

PART III: Planning and Preparing 47

CHAPTER 7: Vision Boards and Goal Orientation: Mapping the Future 50

CHAPTER 8: Mastermind Groups: Mentoring with Peers 56

CHAPTER 9: Accounting and Accountability: Measuring Achievement 62

PART IV: Maintaining Motivation 67

CHAPTER 10: Actionable Tasks: Checklists, Milestones, and Sustainability 70

CHAPTER 11: Finding Your Future: Goals Beyond the Now 75

CHAPTER 12: More Side Hustles for All Types 80

PART V: Inspiring Examples 86

CHAPTER 13: Budding Entrepreneurs: Side Hustle Success Stories 89

    Miss Design Berry: Kristin Berry 89

    Philosophie Group, Inc.: Skot Carruth 90

    Impressa Solutions: Julie T. Ewald.............. 91

    The Amani Experience: Amani Roberts....... 92

    Pet Sitter: Melanie Lewis.............................. 93

CHAPTER 14: Famous Entrepreneurs: Advice from Above 96

CHAPTER 15: Goal Setting for Success 102

Conclusion.. 107

Introduction

Work, school, family, and friends: we all live busy, productive, sometimes hectic lives. Occasionally, it feels that we are simply running in place, just trying to keep up with what we already have on our plates. Unfortunately, the larger goals we have in mind—for creative success, for financial security—often fall by the wayside. Having an action plan to set goals, maintain momentum, and stay motivated to keep meeting milestones is the only sure way to achieve what you deserve. This book will help you identify your goals, capitalize on your passions, and maintain accountability, all while continuing to lead your best life.

First, you must establish your parameters: what are your goals for the future? What is your idea of financial security? Next, you must designate a plan to meet those goals—and, perhaps most importantly, chart a clear path toward accountability in getting there and staying on track. Some ideas to help you supplement your main income with simple—or more involved, depending on your available time and level of desire—side hustles are also outlined throughout.

Finally, we will end with a handful of inspiring stories about busy people, just like you, who were able to achieve great success with a solid idea and no small amount of clear-eyed goals and determination.

Embark upon your journey toward financial security and entrepreneurial success. It takes passion, planning, and careful plotting of progress. Use this book as your compass to charting your course and start setting your goals today!

PART I:
Establishing Your Parameters

"If you want to be happy, set a goal that commands your thoughts, liberates your energy and inspires your hopes."

– Andrew Carnegie

Certainly, one of the most crucial factors in setting goals is to establish your parameters: a goal is the designated end to a set of actions, not something that will merely appear out of thin air. But first, you must determine limits of that goal, the ends to which you will work to meet. People often ask the five-year question—"where do you see yourself in five years?"—which certainly may be helpful, but only in a vague sort of way. Get specific and categorize: what should your finances look like in five, ten, or twenty years? What should your professional life look like? Hours spent working? Retirement at what age? There is also the infamous work-life balance: are your financial goals in line with your life goals? How much time and energy do you wish to spend at home, with family and/or children, or at leisure? What about travel? Establishing parameters for your goals is to look at all aspects of your life—professional, personal, and private (for some, that might also include political, be it activism or actual participation)—and determine what you desire, then set up an action plan to achieve it.

Ideally, establishing parameters is a positive seeking of personal enlightenment. What things do I value the most? And how do I go about getting them? The answers, of course, are nearly infinite. For some, professional success will always be paramount, though this also requires definition: is a success to be measured in money or in recognition or in accomplishing a greater good? For others, personal success will be paramount, in the form of raising a family or pursuing a creative goal. For many, success is an amalgam of the professional and the personal. For still others, goal setting is more important than eventual success: for them, the journey is ultimately worth more than the destination. As well, it must be acknowledged that not all of our goals are within our personal control (such as having children or achieving fame), and it is always better to acknowledge this simple fact at the outset of any plan. That is, any good plan also has a contingent one. For any of the above, however, setting goals within the parameters of your own talents and desires, striving for the highest and best while acknowledging practical limitations is the absolute most crucial part of getting to where you'd like to be.

First, let's investigate the application of smart goals and how to utilize your passion and skills to achieve the success you desire; we are all happier when in pursuit of success to be doing something we love. Next, we will investigate some tools and applications that can help you with this process, as we could all use support and external motivation. Last, we will talk about limitations—time, resources, energy—and how to maintain a balance that will keep you achieving goals and enjoying life to its fullest.

CHAPTER 1:
Passion and Possibilities: SMART Goals

Beyond the obvious necessity of setting clear parameters, goals shouldn't be a frightening or overwhelming burden: they should be avenues to success that inspire and motivate you to achieve. As such, always be ready to pursue your passions in addition to more pragmatic aspirations. The more passionate you are about what you are doing to reach your goals, the more successful you will be in the long run. Or, concomitantly, the more passionate you are about your goals, the abler you will be able to endure what you must work through in order to achieve them. It's worth it to keep an uninspiring job if you are working toward a better—and, more importantly, specifically designated—endpoint. Goals are both pathways to achievement and roadmaps out of dead ends. Either way, setting goals based on your passions and with a clear-eyed vision of the possibilities can lead you to whatever destination you desire.

Not only do you need goals that motivate you, but you also need to prioritize your goal setting. That is, look at the highest and best purposes you wish to achieve and set your goals accordingly. If you set too many goals, then you risk losing focus of the bigger picture. On the other, if the goals you set are too overwhelmingly large, then you risk becoming overwhelmed and leaving them unmet. The best practice is to set goals that are of high priority, broken down into manageable tasks over a reasonable period of time—passionate drive coupled with pragmatic implementation. One quick and easy way to determine if you have this combination right is, first, to answer the question "what is most valuable and meaningful to me?" and, second, to check your answer with a trusted friend or advisor. If reliable others are not convinced that is a worthwhile or practical goal, then it may do to revisit it. This does not mean giving up on hopes and dreams, of course, but it does mean that, on occasion, we may have to check our loftier aspirations against the reality of our situation. I can dream of one day being a wealthy and famous writer, but the reality is that most writers become neither. Still, I can work to achieve that goal one project at a time, with determination and drive—and accept the joys of simply being a working writer. This is part of the balance that is at the core of most goal setting.

One of the best and simplest tools in goal setting is something called SMART goals: this is an acronym for specific, measurable, achievable, relevant, and time-bound. When you clearly define these five concepts for yourself, then you are well on your way to achieving whatever you put your mind to. Let's explore further.

SPECIFIC: The best way to turn your vague hopes and dreams into specific goals is to ask yourself the five "W" questions. What do I hope to achieve? Why is this important to me? Who do I need in order to succeed at this goal? Where do I need to be (physically, perhaps, or otherwise) to succeed? And, which resources do I need, which limitations do I face? Answering each of these questions as simply and specifically as possible is an excellent first step. To use the above example, instead of amorphous terms like "wealthy" and "famous," set goals that define what those terms mean to you. For another example, if your goal is to retire by age 50 so that you can pursue your personal passions (whatever they may be) and have the leisure to time to spend with family and friends, then you've answered the first two questions. Now, you must in your individual context, start to work on answering the rest. This is where some other SMART tips can help.

MEASURABLE: Here is where vague aspirations become concrete manifestations. If your goals are not measurable, then you have no mechanism by which to chart your progress or to stay focused. This is when you ask "how" questions: how much? How many? How will I know that I have achieved the goal I set? To return to the above example, you would calculate just how much money you would need to have saved and/or invested in order to retire at 50, as well as identifying how many years you have to meet that financial number. You would also define what your post-retirement should look like, according to your wishes.

ACHIEVABLE: Now you start to check yourself. If you are 45 years old, then the plan to retire at 50 may not be achievable if you haven't already started working toward it. If you are 35, it becomes more realistically achievable. In either case, you can still achieve the goal, but you must adjust accordingly: the 45-year-old may change the retirement number to 55 and lower the amount they feel they have to save, for example. This also requires some philosophical consideration: early retirement may not be as satisfying as you expect unless you make actionable plans for how you want to spend your time.

RELEVANT: This addresses the final point made above, in part. If you derive meaning and satisfaction from your job, then early retirement may not be the best goal for you. It may sound good because you do want to travel and enjoy leisure time; however, if you lose the feeling that you are productive, then that should give you pause to rethink your ultimate goal. In addition, your goal must also come into alignment with your current situation and others in your life. Are you sure that this is the best pathway for you? How does your goal impact others (for example, sending your grown children to college if you retire early)? How does your goal impact other goals you have?

TIME-BOUND: Any achievable goal should have some sort of deadline. First, determine the final endpoint (retire at age 50), then ask yourself what you should be doing in a year from now to work towards that goal. Then, what should be happening in six months? Then, what should be happening each month? Finally, what should happen today in order to actualize the stated goal? These are manageable increments of time that allow you to chart your progress and measure your success.

CHAPTER 2:
Programs and Apps: Tools for Success

Even the most disciplined among us need assistance in staying on track, and with modern technology, that assistance is usually at your fingertips. Old-fashioned techniques such as journaling or list-making certainly never go out of style, but if you are like most adults today, you always have your smartphone or tablet with you, ready and available to keep you focused and successful.

There are numerous apps available out there, most for free, with different uses for different users. Some of the more popular apps are listed below, along with their attributes.

- **Strides:** this is one of the broadest apps available out there, which will allow you to track daily habits—such as fitness and diet—alongside making budgets and saving money. It also allows you to input your goal and set a specific date for achieving it, sending reminders along the

way. One clear drawback is that it's not available on Android.
- **GoalsOnTrack:** this tool is both web-based and mobile, and it uses the SMART goal formula (see the previous chapter) as its format. It also allows you to break down your goals into manageable pieces and has a journaling feature, as well, which allows you to make notes about your progress. Keeping track of your triumphs and frustrations is an excellent way to plan for future goals. This tool is not free, and there is a web site you must sign up on before you download the app.
- **Way of Life:** this app uses lots of charts and graphs that allow you to chart your daily progress in maintaining (or jettisoning) habits. This is designed for smaller, everyday goals, like losing weight or stopping smoking. You enter in the action you'd like to take (lose weight), then the app sends you daily reminder as to what to do (or not do, if your goal is to stop smoking). The advantage to this app is that, over time, it will show you trends of behavior, giving you more knowledge of what might trigger you to stray from your goals.

- **Coach.me:** another very popular app, this helps you track your daily habits with a virtual life coach; if you like the app a lot, you can upgrade for a fee to an actual personalized coach. You earn rewards for sticking to your goals, and there is a community of users for support and information.
- **ATracker:** This application reveals how you are spending your time on a daily basis. This does not necessarily address goals as themselves, but it shows you how much time you spend doing activities that are geared toward your goals—it helps you make time, not waste time. Over time, you will be able to see your habits by a weekly and monthly basis, allowing you to see the bigger picture of how your habits are leading you to success (or not). There is a free version with a restricted number of tasks to chart.
- **Forest: Stay Focused:** This app helps you to get work done without interruption while using a gaming interface. Basically, you plant a seed that grows into a tree over the time you spend staying focused on a designated task. If you successfully manage not to answer a text or a call for the designated amount of time, then you

will earn coins that will allow you to choose the kind of tree you grow and so on. Or, you can use your coins to donate to Trees for the Future, a non-profit organization that plants actual trees. The app isn't free, but its cost is minimal.
- **Fabulous:** While not cheap, this app is a science-based tool that utilizes experts and data to help keep you on track with daily habits leading to larger goals. You can subscribe monthly or yearly.
- **Habit-Bull:** This flexible application allows you to track your personalized goals in one of several ways, so you can check progress daily or according to your own needs. Users can enable notifications to send reminders, as well. It's free for up to five daily habits, but for a minimal cost, users can upgrade to up to 100 daily tasks.
- **Loop Habit Tracker:** This app is like an electronic checklist, wherein you check items off of your predetermined list and close the loop for a given period of time. Users can also set notifications for specific times. This app is free but is Android only.
- **Streaks:** This app zeroes in on the dozen most pressing activities you want to accomplish in your daily routine. It is integrated with the iOS Health app, as

well, so the data transfers over for easy analysis. Not available for Android.
- **Productive:** Another iPhone specific app, Productive is another that works to track daily habits more than specific goals. It is available for free, but a paid version offers lots more data.
- **Trello:** This app is great for project managers of all types—whether you are managing a household or an office. It tracks not only your to-do list but also those of your family or your team. Recurring reminders and color-coding options allow you to track collaborative progress over time. The free version is great for personal use (planning a vacation, keeping track of family duties), while the paid version is more suited for professional use.

There are also several web-based and software programs that will help you track your goals, among them Goal-Buddy, GoalEnforcer, and Goalscape. These are all designed to help you set and track your goals, with enticing visuals and interactive features. While most of the apps available are geared toward daily activities and habits, these web-based programs are focused on long-term goals and the manageable tasks it takes to get there. Used in tandem with mobile apps, these tools are all useful for anyone who is new to goal setting or has had difficulty with maintaining momentum in the past. Many of these web-based programs are geared towards small business owners, and as we will address later in the book, these tools can be vastly helpful in setting up and maintaining a successful side hustle. Certainly, though, any of these tools can assist you in keeping track of your life in the midst of the hustle and bustle of the everyday.

CHAPTER 3:
Limits and Learning:
Keeping Balance

We regularly hear about the need to attain an ideal work-life balance—and regularly hear why it is near impossible to do. Be that as it may, the concept of maintaining a work-life balance is a goal in and of itself. In addition, keeping balance in your life is imperative for the attaining of goals; without momentum, you will inevitably fall behind, but without joy and leisure, you will inevitably burn out. So, when setting your goals—particularly when setting time frames for actualizing them—be sure to keep in mind a healthy balance between what you need to do, what you have to do, and what you'd like to do. All of these things are important for overall happiness.

Certainly, the right balance for you is not necessarily the right balance for anyone else and vice versa. Understand your own needs in the context of your personal and professional goals to determine what is best for your situation. Acknowledging your limitations, whatever they are, is the first best step towards not losing your way: if you push too hard to reach a difficult goal, forsaking everything else, then you often set yourself up to fail. Follow some of these simple tips to keep your eye on the proverbial prize.

First, since you are reading this book, one can make the assumption that you are interested in setting and keeping goals—this may because you haven't motivated yourself to do so in the past and need some advice, OR it could be because you have done this kind of thing before but it hasn't quite worked out. In either case, one of the first things that you have to do when setting attainable goals and still maintaining your busy life is to *let go of perfection*. While setting specific goals is important, and holding yourself accountable to daily progress and deadlines equally so, it should not be so onerous that you lose sight of the bigger picture amid the minute details of the day today. Keep things in context, as well. If your greatest goal is to save money for early retirement, then obviously you'll be keeping close track of your finances. But if you decide to meet friends for a quick drink that turns into dinner and a night out on the town—you've overextended your daily budget—don't panic and don't berate yourself. Just don't make it a daily habit. It's one day, and you certainly deserve to have some leisure time on occasion. The important thing here is not to hold yourself to the highest standard every moment of every day—that's exhausting!

Second, one of the greatest time destroyers that most adults face is that of the inevitable pull of technology. All of the apps mentioned in the previous chapter are excellent tools for helping keep you on track, of course, and smartphones and email and DVR devices are inherently useful and entertaining—and here to stay. Yet, we often find ourselves mindlessly using these bits of technology without realizing how much time we are on them. In addition, if work is added to the mix—say, if you telecommute for your daily job—then these devices can hold a tyrannical grip on your life. Keeping track of your productive time is important for setting and achieving goals; so is keeping track of your downtime, your ability to recharge, just like your phone must.

Third, whatever goal(s) you wish to achieve in your life, you should always have in mind that health and well-being is an often unspoken one—and it shouldn't be! If your goal is to save money for early retirement, as in our earlier examples, then your focus is on financial planning. However, an attendant goal should be feeling good enough to enjoy that retirement when you get there. So, keeping track of daily exercise and engaging in healthy activities—as many of the apps discussed in the previous chapter will help you do—is absolutely paramount. There is also something to be said for meditation, time spent to help you detach and unwind from the hectic pace around you. Centering yourself can give you more motivation to be more active the next day. Exercise has the added benefit of not only keeping your body healthy but it also keeps your mind sharp. This kind of personal time does not get in the way of you attaining your goals; rather, it is value-added time that aids you in your progress.

Fourth, prioritize, prioritize, and prioritize! Into everyone's life, a few time-wasting encounters must fall, but we must be keen to recognize them and work to avoid them. This goes for everything from surfing the internet to binge-watching mediocre television. This isn't to say that you avoid those activities, it's to say you devote those to set periods of time (this is why you can set your smartphone to turn itself off after a certain period of use), or to more qualitative experiences. If you watch three episodes of a show that you just kind of enjoy, then release yourself from feeling obligated to watch the next nine. This also applies to colleagues and relationships: there are times when we must be self-aware (not selfish) that our time is important, and mindless chatter around the water cooler or via text doesn't accomplish much.

Fifth, you can achieve your goals and a healthy work-life balance with some restructuring of your daily life and habits (again, the previous chapter gives you some tools with which to start). Other than paying attention to your time, as discussed above, you might consider some of the things that you do in your life that have become routine but don't necessarily need to be so. Outsource when you can, or delegate some responsibilities to spouse, partner, or children of adequate age. Change to routine is always hard, but it might just save your goal from landing on the ash heap of history.

Sixth, don't overreach. As discussed in Chapter 2, SMART goals are realistic goals, and efficient people who achieve them most often do so by breaking them down into manageable components, rather than overwhelming wholes. As the old canard goes, how does one eat an elephant? One satisfying bite at a time.

PART II:
Achieving Financial Goals

*"Be practical as well as
generous in your ideals.
Keep your eyes on the stars,
but remember to keep your
feet on the ground."*

– Theodore Roosevelt

One of the most important long-term goals you can set is that of financial security. This is often something that many of us don't think about until it's too late to achieve exactly what we'd like. This is why it's crucial not only to define what your long-term idea of solvency and security is but also how to get there through realistic and manageable goals.

The first hurdle is in determining what matters most to you. When setting financial goals, begin by putting everything on the table, from your most grandiose hopes to your most pragmatic realities—then sort through this to determine what is truly possible based on your current situation. Divide up your goals into the immediate (do I need to change my current situation to have any hope of reaching my goals?), the short-term (open a savings account), and the long-term (invest). Use the SMART goals techniques discussed in Chapter 2 for some assistance. Finally, the trick is to monitor your progress in a consistent and careful manner.

One of the most strikingly simple financial goals you can set is that of setting a budget: this can be weekly, monthly, and even daily—whatever best fits your needs. It may not be possible to stick to your budget always—there are always unexpected emergencies or surprises—but it is certainly extraordinarily helpful in order to track your spending habits over time. Another simple goal you can work towards is setting up an emergency fund; this will help you to keep within your budget, come what may. Most financial experts also urge that you pay off your debt as quickly as you can as often as you can. Credit card debt, especially, can eat away at even the most well-intentioned budget and savings. There are some who also suggest that, depending on your financial goals, you strive to live *below* your means. This is a trend among millennials today who are looking toward early retirements and pursuing personal passions rather than spending their disposable income on newer cars or larger homes. Again, what you decide to do depends on what your specific goals are.

The following chapters will focus on some different ways in which you can set up your financial goals. First, deciding on how much you need for how long is crucial to any long-term goal, and any short-term decisions you make with regard to your finances will impact that significantly. Next, opportunities for increasing your earning power, while still keeping your primary employment, have never been more prolific. We will discuss the burgeoning world of side hustles. Last, once you have developed a side hustle, you must learn to market it and manage it in order to maximize its earning potential. With some of these new ideas and flexible opportunities, achieving financial security is certainly within your grasp.

CHAPTER 4:
Determining Your Future: What Do You Need

To set realistic long-term goals is a difficult task: it is hard to determine exactly what you will need throughout your retirement years. Predicting the future is an impossible task for anyone. However, there are some actionable steps you can take to ensure that you are prepared for what may come. Deciding on your long-term goals is, obviously, the first step: how much do you need to live comfortably now? How much will you need to meet your goals for retirement in the future? Discussing these issues with a financial planner is always a sound idea, but there are some simple ways in which you can personally set yourself up for success.

As already mentioned in the forward to this section, there are some very simple steps that anyone can follow to attain financial security, such as budgeting, saving, and paying down debt. Budgeting sounds so simple that it is surprising how few people do it with consistent regularity. One easy formula to help you focus on sensible budgeting is the 50/20/30 rule: basically, break down your income into percentages, 50% going to needs like rent or mortgage, utilities, insurance, and so on. The next 20% should go to your savings and, eventually, investments. Finally, the last 30% can then go to your "wants," like eating out, shopping, and traveling. This is a sensible and achievable balance for most securely employed people.

When it comes to saving, there are some quick tricks you can utilize to help keep you on the straight and narrow. First and foremost, almost all employers offer the option to send your direct deposit to more than one account: have a portion of your paycheck sent to savings each pay period. This will ensure that you don't simply forget or overspend without thinking about savings first. You can also increase your savings by being frugal with your disposable income, cutting back on your cable bill or your phone's data plan. Buying groceries and cooking at home saves a great deal of money over time, and curbing extraneous shopping habits is an excellent way to ensure that your future is secure. Depending on your goals, it might be more important to spend the extra time required in cooking at home rather than spending the money to eat out. It's also prudent to think through large purchases at length: do you really need a new car if your current one is still in fine working condition?

These kinds of simple consideration can increase your savings quickly.

Other items that you can easily automate in order to keep your budget breakdown in check are bills and investments. Choosing autopay for your bills is an excellent idea, especially if you are steadily and securely employed. This ensures that your budget doesn't go awry, as well as avoids the possibilities of late payments which might affect your overall credit score. In addition, if you are investing some of your income—a good idea, and one that many experts can guide you through—you can automate that, as well, using one of several apps (such as Acorn) to assist you. Finally, you can also set any loans you may have to autopay, another surefire way to keep budgeting on track.

Paying down debt is also a sure-fire way to keep you on track for meeting long-term financial goals. Not only does this keep your income from going to high-interest rates, but it also boosts your credit scores, which in turn gets you better interest rates for future purchases. Getting out of debt also has the added benefits of alleviating the stress associated with constant money woes, as well as giving you more control over the income that you have. Indeed, getting out of debt and having a savings account allows you freedom and flexibility in the short-term, as well—quitting an unsatisfying job is possible if you have that cushion, for example. Quitting a job without having other prospects available isn't the wisest of ideas, of course, but the idea of feeling in control over your destiny is an attractive one, and getting out of debt is one in which to achieve that sense.

In addition to a savings account, many financial advisors suggest that you build up an emergency fund. This fund should have about three months of essential expenses built into it. This prevents a minor emergency from turning into a long-term financial disaster. Certainly, this is more difficult than creating quick savings account for the occasional splurge (holiday spending, for example), but it is another cushion that keeps you on the path to long-term financial solvency.

Another very practical piece of advice is to read up on personal finance. There are numerous books that detail the pathways to financial success via multiple routes. This also keeps you current on financial practices and tips to help you invest even more in your future.

Something else to consider which many of us do not until it is too late: keep your health goals front and center, as well. The financial impact of poor health can be devastating, of course, but even the simplest lifestyle changes can avoid certain diseases and the expensive medications that go along with them. Eating healthy and exercising, quitting smoking, and drinking in moderation are all things that can keep you from persistent conditions like diabetes, heart disease, and cancer. There are even apps out there that will pay you to lose weight, should you need to—the catch is that you will owe them if you are unable to reach your goals. For some, this may be just the motivation to get them going.

Finally, if you are employed in a steady, secure, and lucrative job or career, but you still find that you would like to increase your financial portfolio for the future, there are possibilities for extra income out there right now that has been unsurpassed in recent years. The growing trend of the side hustle has exploded in recent years, with some reports suggesting that nearly half of all American adults engage in one in some form or another. These can range from the basic (selling items on eBay) to the involved (blogging, YouTube channel). You can generate anywhere from a couple of hundred dollars a month to thousands. In the next chapter, these new avenues to financial security and success will be discussed at length.

CHAPTER 5:
New Avenues to Success: The Side Hustle

The side hustle is a way in which those of us who wish to earn more, save more, or both can invest a little time and energy to make a bit more cash on the side. If you already have a full-time job and a busy life, then it can be difficult to envision how you would have the time and energy left to direct to another form of employment. This is the beauty of the side hustle—very little commitment (in most cases) and enormous flexibility (in all cases). You can decide how much or how little time you invest, and especially if you are already gainfully employed, you can walk away at any time. The other unexpected advantage of a side hustle is that, in some cases, the side hustle can develop into a full-blown business opportunity in and of itself. There are countless examples of young entrepreneurs taking their side hustle into an enormously successful business (we will take a look at some of these people and their businesses in Part V). Engaging in a side hustle is a lucrative opportunity of varying degrees for anyone who wishes to increase their income or to pursue a passion while maintaining everyday stability.

There are some basic rules to embarking on a side hustle, especially if that side gig is secondary to a full-time career. There are many people out there who take a side hustle because they can only find part-time work, and there are some who take on more than one side hustle to cobble together a shaky income. For the purposes of this chapter, the assumption will be that you are reading this in order to increase a steady, stable income with an eye toward earning more, saving more, and achieving greater long-term financial security and success.

First and foremost, the side hustle shouldn't interfere with your success in your primary employment. This will be the first consideration when determining what kind of side hustle you might like to try; if it takes too much time or energy that it detracts from your stable income (remember: there is no health insurance in the side hustle), then it isn't for you. Compromising your productivity at your day job is not an advisable way in which to net any long-term gains.

In light of the above advice, another pitfall to avoid is taking on debt as a result of the side hustle. Again, this advice goes toward choosing the right side hustle for you. Basically, this means that you don't get ahead of yourself and start investing in a start-up that has no proven record. If your ultimate goal is to start an entrepreneurial business, then start with a side hustle in that field in which you don't have to invest. Get some experience and knowledge of what works and what doesn't work. Save your side hustle money until you have enough to invest in your own venture. Also, beware of using a side hustle venture as an excuse to spend inordinate amounts of time on a hobby. Certainly, we all like mucking about in the garden or garage, but without a clear business plan and proven success, these kinds of businesses often fail. Also, be sure not to work on a side hustle that creates a conflict of interest with your day job; there is nothing but an ill will to be gained from creating a source of direct conflict.

One of the best ways to get started is to determine what it is that interests you. For some of us, this is immediately clear: he's always had a passion for metalworking; she's always loved to write. For others of us, taking the time to think about what would drive you to spend more hours working is worth it. Only something that you feel truly passionate about can keep you interested in and focused on your progress in that arena.

Crucially important to the entrepreneurial side hustle is the time factor. Be certain that you create a set schedule and stick to it. Not only do you not want to shortchange your primary employer, but you also don't want to shortchange yourself or your family. Know and acknowledge your limitations before you quickly burn out.

There are literally hundreds of side hustles that are out there for the taking right now. Following is a list of some side hustles, beginning with the fairly involved (for those who are seeking entrepreneurial avenues) to the simple task for extra cash.

- Set up a dropshipping business: this kind of side hustle will enable you to capitalize on nearly any interest you may have, from fashion and makeup to home décor to science fiction memorabilia. Basically, this gig allows you to buy direct from a manufacturer and ship to your customer, no brick and mortar store necessary. Your primary concerns will be marketing and building a customer base (more on that in the next chapter).
- Try your hand at affiliate marketing: this is where you guide online visitors to a website to buy products, earning a commission from each sale. Beware that a lot of people who try their hand at this end up making not much or nothing; choose

the product and brand well to have the best chance at success. If you are already good at marketing, this side hustle has great potential.
- If you happen to be good at writing, then there are many ways you can monetize your skill. If you're a good writer with a talent for self-promotion, then you can be even more successful. Freelance writing offers opportunities to make extra money by writing articles or longer works for various places. CraigsList offers an opportunity for you to start gathering clients, but there are various companies online who are looking for freelance writers regularly. There is also blogging, of course, which is a riskier venture in terms of income; blogging brings in nothing at first, but with time, effort, passion, and marketing, a successful blogger can make good money. Creating a personalized niche is the first step to a successful blog, and it helps to affiliate it with a website that doubles as a virtual store. Combining content with commerce is a typically successful way for bloggers to gain traction.
- Another growing side hustle is that of a virtual assistant, which is exactly what it

sounds like: you provide support services to an individual or organization from a remote location. Virtual assistants specialize in numerous areas, such as social media, bookkeeping, and administrative duties. Sites like Upwork help you find clients for this kind of side hustle, though you will inevitably make more money by being an independent contractor. As with most entrepreneurial gigs, start small, gain skills and confidence, then branch out.

- Finally, you can join what is being called the "gig economy," wherein you trade your time for money as an independent contractor in short-term gigs. An old school example would be a musician, who is paid for his or her "gig" at the club over a night or a contractual series of nights. More contemporary examples are Uber and Lyft, Airbnb, TaskRabbit, Etsy, and so on. These gigs simply require your time and (sometimes) skill set, and you take on only the jobs you want when you want. These side hustles aren't intended to be long-term stable employment; however, there are instances when a gig turns into an opportunity.

This is just a general overview of some of the many, many side's hustles that are available out there for busy working people who have an interest in setting aside a little more cash each month in savings, investing a bit more for the future, or in pursuing a passion into a potential entrepreneurial opportunity. There are literally hundreds of examples out there, and we will continue to explore these in the following chapter and beyond.

CHAPTER 6:
Marketing and the Side Hustle: Specific Targets

Now that you have started a side hustle—or are considering how to jump in at least for the short-term—the marketing aspect of the business becomes paramount for meeting any financial goals you may have set for it. Again, if you are merely embarking on a casual side hustle as a way to be able to put a little bit more money into savings, then setting yourself up with a side gig is the way to go. However, if you are interested in pursuing a side hustle that can eventually end up earning significant amounts of money, even becoming a business in its own right, then you will eventually have to think about marketing itself.

Fundamentally, marketing these days is technology-based, from social media to web sites to email, but there are also traditional forms of marketing (word-of-mouth, for one powerful example) that can build your idea into an empire. Let's examine some of the more significant marketing tools that can help you grow your side hustle into something lucrative.

Obviously, social media has been one of the most influential presences in our lives for the past decade, despite some growing concerns with aspects of privacy. With regard to a side hustle that you wish to grow, it is still yet fairly imperative that you create a social media presence in order to both network and advertise. Clearly, Facebook and Twitter are the reigning champions of social media, but Instagram comes in handy especially if your side hustle involves anything that you can visually market (crafts, flowers, food, jewelry, fashion). LinkedIn is another social media site that also allows for professional networking.

Beyond a social media presence, it is a good idea to set up your own web site. People may find out about your business/service via social media but often will want to learn more details about it via a web site. A web site also offers more personalization and more variety in terms of how you market your product—and yourself. Remember that marketing is oftentimes, especially in the entrepreneurial spirit, about marketing yourself as much as what brand you are trying to build. Building a web site in today's technologically saturated world is surprisingly easy, with various sites to help you along the way that cost little to nothing to you. There are also tutorials galore on YouTube and other platforms to help you develop a fun, interesting, and engaging site.

Some truly effective old-fashioned ways of marketing your side hustle include business cards and person-to-person networking. Business cards are also cheap and easy to come by these days, with several online services offering personalized designs at a reasonable cost. These are handy notecards to remind people of your presence and how to get in touch with you; they serve as convenient conversation pieces to start a pitch, should you find yourself in a scenario in which that's appropriate. If so, be sure you know what you'd say to someone who is in a position to show genuine interest—and potential investment—in your idea or fledgling company. Make sure you have a quick and clear synopsis, as well as a concept of what your ultimate goal might be.

Word-of-mouth networking is still, even in this digital age, an extremely effective way to get people interested in what you have to say and to sell. Think about how to expand your networking beyond your personal set of family and friends. Essentially, successfully politicians—especially at the local level—are simply very skilled at personal networking. Regardless of how you feel about politics, some of those skills can be valuable at many levels. In addition, check into work-sharing spaces, another growing trend in the side hustle economy, wherein there is a built-in network as well as space for you to work without investing too much money.

There are also marketing opportunities that themselves can become side hustles. If it turns out that you happen to be good at marketing products or services, then you can use those skills either to invest and grow your own business or to assist others while making some money yourself. In the second instance, your investment is merely one of time, so it is an excellent option for talented marketers who don't necessarily want to incur the personal risk of starting a business. The following examples are both opportunities to take advantage of when marketing products or ways in which you can provide services to another individual or organization.

Platforms such as Google's AdWords help businesses optimize their search results. This is a savvy investment as your business picks up, and a valuable skill to learn if you have experience with digital marketing. There is also social media advertising management, wherein you pay someone to manage ad campaigns for your product or business; again, if you have marketing skills already, this is a side hustle that you can do yourself for other businesses. Native advertising is another marketing tool that can be useful, wherein a business can post sponsored content to another individual's or company's web site while appearing native to the site itself (that is, it's hard to see the difference between the advertising and the main content). And, in the days of social media influencers, reaching out to them about your product or service can gain you valuable traction—not an easy task, for sure, but one to consider.

Last, don't forget about traditional advertising altogether. While many of us get much of our information and do a lot of our commerce online, there are still advantages to marketing in print or other traditional forms. If you are providing a service to a small community in particular, then traditional newspaper ads, flyers, or local magazines provide a valuable source of visibility. Let us not forget that one of the intensely successful rallying cry of the last decade or so has been "local"; the cache of the local that goes viral has been a markedly noticeable shift in commercial ventures today, from food to artisanal products to handmade goods.

PART III:
Planning and Preparing

"It must be borne in mind that the tragedy of life doesn't lie in not reaching your goal. The tragedy lies in having no goals to reach."

– Benjamin E. Mays

One of the crucial keys to any successful goal setting is specific and detailed planning. As we have often been told, poor preparation leads to poor performance (leaving out the salty language). That other timeworn adage, expect the best and prepare for the worst, is also a canard worth listening to. From the short-term to the long-term, goals require clear vision, constant vigilance, and proper preparation. By following all of the tips and techniques discussed in the first three chapters, you are well on your way to defining and reaching your goals. Now, work to stay focused and accountability for meeting each step along the way to the ultimate goal.

There are some basic rules for the most successful goal setting. First, the goals you set must, in the end, be ones that motivate you; if you aren't driven to reach the goal, then no amount of planning or oversight can get you from point A to point Z. This doesn't mean that having an off day or a bad week will derail all of your hopes and dreams—we all have struggles with which to contend—it simply means that if a goal is important to you, you will get back on track quickly after you stumble. It also means that you will put in the hard work, effort, and discipline that will eventually get you there.

Second, as we have already discussed (Chapter 2), use the SMART goal method to set specific, measurable, attainable, relevant, and time-bound goals. Third, put your goals in writing: this can be in the form of a journal or a chart, on a calendar traditional or digital, on a web site platform or mobile app. Wherever you feel most comfortable operating doesn't matter; what matters is that you put the goal into clear and coherent writing, with action plans and deadlines in place. This is powerful not just because you have made a commitment (albeit still an abstract one) but because it begins to take shape and feel more tangible and possible when you see it concretely. Keeping goals in your head limits them to vague hopes and dreams; writing them down, planning them out and creating a mechanism for accountability makes them realistic goals. Be sure you make a clearly defined action plan, as well as prepare for ways in which you continue to chart your progress.

Some specific ways to map out your goals are explored in the next three chapters. Vision boards and task orientation are ways to chart your progress visually, as well as to hold you accountable to keep up with your deadlines. There are also mastermind groups, wherein you will be held accountable by others, as well. You also need to prepare for how you will measure your achievements and when you will know that a set goal has been reached.

CHAPTER 7:
Vision Boards and Goal Orientation: Mapping the Future

Vision boards are the adult version of the collage we made back in school talking about what we want to be when we grow up. These visual collages are empowering and immediate reminders of what we are aiming for and how we intend to get there. Goal orientation is a mindset that removes you from the relentless rut of focusing on repetitive tasks and instead orients you to the goal-fulfilling future. Both of these tools are visual and psychological assistants toward mapping your goals, keeping track of them, and ultimately reaching them.

The inspirational nature of a vision board is hard to overstate. These are tools that are used across many organizations and serve as powerful reminders of what is at stake in what we do each and every day. Creating a vision board is intensely personal: this is *your* vision and yours alone, with materials, images, and icons that serve to motivate each action you take. Once you have set your sights on a SMART—specific, measurable attainable, relevant, and time-bound—goal and put it in writing, then make a visual representation of this with your vision board and place it somewhere that you can see it every day. Visual images are emotionally potent, and here is where the psychological aspect of goal setting comes into play. Logical tools are important, but so is the emotional pull of visualizing and revisiting your dreams, tangible reminders of why you are putting in the time, effort, and discipline to reach said goal.

Find an appropriate material on which to create your vision board: anything from your basic poster board to a sturdier foam-backed base will serve as your starting point. Write your goal(s) somewhere clearly on the board where it will serve as a daily prompt to get you up and running. Collect a bunch of magazines with colorful and inspirational pictures; cut out those images to paste onto your vision board. These images do not have to align exactly with your stated goal, but they should make you *feel* strongly about what you want. When you come across something that makes you say "*this* is what I want my life to look like," that's when you know you've come across inspiration to get you working toward your goal. Arrange these pictures on your board in any pattern pleasing to you.

Once you have an aesthetically pleasing arrangement of inspirational images, consider adding a picture of yourself in order to represent your presence amid these dreams in a tangible way. Write affirmative quotations or sayings or concepts next to or directly onto the images themselves. Be sure to include purely emotional feelings—this is most definitely the place when the logic of goal-setting is secondary to the crucial aspect of emotional attachment. Words such as joy, happiness, fulfillment, strong, and free all push powerful emotional buttons; think about how you will feel once you have accomplished your goal. We are motivated more by emotion than by logic; logic is what gets us to accomplish the tasks that lead to emotional fulfillment. Be sure to put your vision board in a place of prominence for you (not everyone has to see it: a closet is an excellent place where you will see it daily but it remains a personal thing) and take some time to contemplate it every day. Doing this at the beginning of the day will often give you the strength to carry out the action needed to reach fulfillment.

Once you have the inspiration to start your day, you need to turn to practical action to turn your dreams into reality. There is much debate about the difference between a task-oriented personality and a goal-oriented personality. A task-oriented personality gets bogged down in everyday tasks in order to reach a particular goal—this can be advantageous for success, but it can lead to short-term unhappiness, the feeling of drudging through a set of activities while constantly waiting for something else. A goal-oriented person, on the other hand, accomplishes the same tasks, by and large, but does so through the vision of the bigger picture. The focus takes a long view rather than a narrow one; companies employ goal-oriented management styles to realize long-term projects. Personally, it's a way to connect the immediate tasks you are doing to a larger sense of accomplishment. Goal-oriented tasks keep you organized and help you maintain accountability.

A key component toward reaching goals successfully is to break down those goals into manageable pieces. To that end, there are some organizational strategies that highly successful people uniformly use. For example, keep a calendar—or three—with to-do lists and other time-saving reminders of tasks that need to be completed on a deadline. For some, myself included, keeping a wall calendar with family-focused items on it, a desk calendar with work-related items on it, and a digitized calendar for appointment reminders and scheduling works very efficiently. For others, keeping everything on one calendar—using tricks such as color-coding—works better. Whatever your style, this is one of the positive habits that can have huge long-term dividends. In terms of goal setting, it makes sense to have a calendar for daily tasks, a monthly calendar for charting mid-range progress, and a yearly calendar for keeping up with crucial deadlines.

Basically, first you must get organized, and then you must plan. Breaking down large projects into manageable pieces is always good advice in maintaining momentum on the way to a goal. A weekly goal may consist of running ten miles; ticking off two miles a day for five days in the week keeps you consistent and motivated. Finally, don't forget about why you started on this journey in the first place—this is where your vision board becomes as helpful as your indispensable planner.

Some other helpful pieces of advice to keep one goal-oriented and focused are shedding two unhelpful habits: multitasking and saying yes to everything. In the first case, in study after study, multitasking has been revealed to be an enormously wasteful way of trying to accomplish specific tasks. Your focus is scattered, your work becomes slipshod, and you lose the ability to prioritize. We all have to juggle things in our lives all of the time—work, family, leisure—which means that we don't have the mental energy to work between six different spreadsheets at a time. Prioritize your projects, then give due attention to each one in turn. You will be more productive and efficient for doing so.

Also learn how to say no, a problem for many of us, particularly early in our careers and our relationships. For some, it can feel like a signal of weakness if we cannot take on everything; for others, it feels like impoliteness not to simply acquiesce to all that might be asked of us. But if you are truly committed to achieving outstanding goals, then you must learn to diplomatically step aside at certain moments. Last, stay motivated by tracking your progress and engaging in positive thinking: more on these in Part IV.

CHAPTER 8:
Mastermind Groups: Mentoring with Peers

Mastermind groups bring people together to improve their goal achieving abilities in both their professional and personal lives. These groups provide education, brainstorming, mentoring, and support for their individual members. All members work in tandem to challenge each other to set strong goals and—more importantly—to meet them. For many, mastermind groups have been a key part of the process in learning to set and to keep goals.

Basically, these groups function are a default catalyst to accountability. Not only do members help each other to set goals, but they also encourage members to seek higher and higher goals, pushing them to the limits of their potential. As well, the group holds each member accountable for their action plans to meet the goals. Essentially, when you join a mastermind group, you have people to whom you are accountable—an excellent motivator for many people looking to achieve success.

A facilitator oversees the group, offering advice and managing discussion forums. Finding a strong leader is key to the success of the overall group, and a facilitator should be engaged and impartial. Each meeting has a clear agenda, set by the facilitator. Members brainstorm ideas, then set goals and agendas; once you begin to implement your plan, you can bring your problems—and your success stories—to the group, where assistance is offered when needed. Basically, being a part of a mastermind group requires commitment, honesty, and confidentiality. Members play both "devil's advocate" and a supportive colleague.

Joining a mastermind group is not like taking a class: the facilitator is just that, not a teacher or a coach. Each member has an equal voice and shares in the giving and receiving of feedback. The purpose of a mastermind group is not to network—though sharing of resources does often happen—but rather to help all members actualize a plan to meet a specific goal, with support and feedback from the group as a whole. There are numerous places online that offer mastermind group services. Research them carefully to find the best fit for you.

While mastermind groups are primarily about individual members seeking support in creating an action plan and sticking to it, there are also activities that the facilitator or member might suggest in order to motivate members into high gear. Some examples of mastermind group activities follow.

- You might launch a 30-day challenge to get members to meet one big goal within that time frame. As the primary purpose of the group is accountability, there would be daily check-ins to monitor progress. Incentivize this with a desirable reward for those who fulfill the terms of their commitment.
- Depending on how large the group is, you might devote some meeting time to subgroups wherein three or four people are interested in brainstorming one particular idea, such as social media advertising or learning dropshipping as a side hustle or focusing on work-life balance issues. This is a way in which the group can be more responsive to each member's specific needs.
- Sometimes, a group will devote part of its time to studying a particular text or thinker whose ideas have value to the goals the group is trying to attain. We all know that reading an advice book has merit, but when we do it as an individual,

we can often simply leave it at that: good advice, now I'll move on. When you study work in a group setting, you get different perspectives on what's there, of course, but you also can hold each other accountable for implementing some of the changes advocated.

- Belonging to a mastermind group has other advantages, as well: each member will bring something of his or her own expertise to the group. One excellent way to utilize meeting time is to have each individual member have an allotted span of time to teach other members about their expertise. This kind of one-on-one education is invaluable, as well as learning about skills that you might want to acquire.
- While it is not necessary to have an overarching mission statement for the group itself, it might be worthwhile to come up with some sort of vision. What is the purpose of the group? What values does the group want to uphold and/or develop? What is the short-term and long-term plan for the group as a whole?
- Mastermind groups will hold Hot Seat sessions during meetings, for one member to explain their situation—the goal, the

obstacles, the progress, and so on. Then each member gets a chance to respond, while the member in the Hot Seat must listen silently without objection or defense. This allows for open discussion and the free brainstorming of ideas, unleashing problem-solving tools all around. When you set time limits on them—ten minutes for the member in the Hot Seat—you force members to clarify their vision and distill its essence into clear, concise terms. Just the preparation itself is useful in maintaining an action plan and reaching a goal successfully.

- Some groups may even organize a weekend retreat, should this be possible for its members. The facilitator should take on the role of creating a specific agenda for a productive and interactive retreat.

The reasons for joining a mastermind group are numerous and beneficial for the right person. You will be a member of an exclusive group—there is usually an application process—with particular kinds of expertise to share. You will be mentored and advised by those experts, and the group itself is a collaboration with success as its ultimate goal. You will meet people who will help you extend your network of colleagues across time. You will learn new things and be challenged to think in different ways. Finally, joining a mastermind group will always encourage you to think bigger, as you are encouraged to stretch your boundaries and broaden your goals.

CHAPTER 9:
Accounting and Accountability: Measuring Achievement

Now that you have some tools to help you achieve financial goals, shift the focus to how to keep up with the accounting. As we have already addressed, achieving financial goals includes a combination of short-term goals—budgeting, paying down debt, creating an emergency fund—and long-term goals, such as estimating what you'll need for your retirement years. Let's look at what you might need to consider for a long-term plan such as retirement, and then examine some ways to increase that income over time.

In order to figure out how much you might need for retirement, you must decide on how much income you need per annum, then at what age you intend to retire. Your short-term budgetary goals should guide you in this manner; you'll need roughly the same when you retire, adjusting for inflation and other potential lifestyle changes. Also be sure to think about long-term health care costs, as well; these may get more expensive as you get older, of course. Then, consider all the income you will have coming in from Social

Security and any retirement funds that you have already set up. Subtract that from what you think you will need for X amount of retirement years. What's left is how much you need to save. Knowing how much longer you have until retirement indicates how much you need to save and/or invest in the intervening years until then. A good rule of thumb is to save between ten and fifteen percent of every paycheck (ideally, into a 401(k) or IRA account). This long-term goal sets you up for making short-term goals as discussed in previous chapters. Using accountability tools as discussed in Chapter 3 can help you meet monthly goals, as well. The security that accompanies having this preparation is doubtless a goal in and of itself.

Now that you have determined what you need for the future, and you have an action plan in place, what more can you do to supplement that income? Essentially, you have a baseline amount prepared, but it certainly couldn't hurt to try to save or earn more, in case of emergency or simply for additional benefit. As previously discussed, side hustles are a source of additional income, both for those who wish to bring in a bit of extra money and for those who wish to try something riskier and work towards entrepreneurship. In the next section, more side hustles will be discussed, as well.

Still, there are other ways to pursue income, and there are two basic kinds of income to consider: active income versus passive income. Active income is money that you earn indirect payment for work or services rendered: your job is active income; a side hustle can be active income; paid consulting is active income. These are all the ways in which you are trading your time for money, whether it is through salary, hourly, or contract.

Passive income, on the other hand, is income that comes in from assets you already own. This could be a side business, for example, or from rental properties that you own, or sales of products you create or curate. Other examples include income from investments, of course, and things like affiliate income or royalties from product sales (like books or patents). Basically, these are all things that do not require your direct involvement, for the most part: you put your money in a CD and the (minimal) interest it earns is passive income, for one example. Passive income almost always requires a large investment of resources upfront—saving enough money to put into a CD or to buy a property or to write a book—but oftentimes that investment is worth it in the long run. Ideally, you will depend on a combination of active and passive income to get you to and through retirement.

The problem, as with many goals we set, is how to manage time effectively. Any time spent investing in potential passive income is time taken away from active income that you could make right now. Basically, the question becomes what should I focus on right now? There are cases for emphasis on either, depending on your situation.

The case for more active income is usually driven by an immediate need—that money is necessary for day to day expenses—but it can also be driven by a desire to reach a long-term financial goal, such as a more financially comfortable retirement. Most side hustles generate active income quickly and without much personal investment other than time. Joining a ridesharing company, for example, could earn you extra money when you are not busy with your day job—a lot of people have been doing this for years now. Buying and selling products on a site such as Craigslist can also be a quick way to garner active income.

Still, eventually you want to invest some of that time and effort into creating something that will give you passive income: if you're putting in extra hours driving for Uber, then putting that money into a CD or rolling into a retirement account will create passive income via interest collected. Or, should you have a talent for technology and a passion for a particular topic, invest in a web site that can be monetized. Should you have a talent for writing and a worthy topic about which to write, compose a book that can collect royalties. As Warren Buffet allegedly said, "If you don't find a way to make money while you sleep, you will work until you die."

The trick is to find a balance in spending time actively earning while setting up the potential for passive income. If you are interested in engaging in the side hustle, then a split of 75% time and effort towards stable, active income with 25% going to the side hustle is a good way to start to conceive of it. In any case, always keep your eye on the ultimate goal—for motivation and for decision-making—and keep track of how you're spending your time and what you're doing with your income. Planning and preparing need to be followed up and monitored closely with accountability.

PART IV:
Maintaining Motivation

*"It's harder to stay on top
than it is to make the climb.
Continue to seek new goals."*

– Pat Summitt

Often, we start a project or plan a goal with unbridled enthusiasm, only to see that dissipate over time, as we become distracted or overwhelmed. We have discussed how to set goals, alongside some valuable tools to help us maintain accountability, yet we still have to somehow find a way to stay motivated beyond months two or three. We also have to acknowledge that there may be times when our focus is interrupted, our lives disrupted by circumstances beyond our control: when this happens, the best response is to accept it, deal with it head-on, and return to your action plan as soon as you can—rather than wallow in guilt at time lost. It is much better to get back on track even if your original deadline might be missed than to simply give up altogether.

Part of the secret to maintaining motivation is in the goal itself. Like the old saying, "a pound of prevention is worth an ounce of cure," your motivation should be in preventing distraction. The best way to do this is to seek worthy and realistic goals, plan carefully, hold yourself accountable, and tick off milestones as you go. Much of this we have already covered throughout, but it bears repeating: if you are passionate about your goal, then you will be equally passionate about sticking to it. Likewise, if you have a realistic and manageable action plan, then you are much more likely to keep up and maintain the momentum. Setting a goal to lose twenty pounds in a month's time is likely to fail; it's unrealistic and ultimately frustrating. Trying to pay down your debt in six months may also be unrealistic, depending on your situation. Momentum is earned by being able to meet realistic expectations, and the fulfillment that you get once you check off a task or a milestone on your calendar or in your journal gives you the motivation and confidence to continue—even if (especially if!) it is challenging. A reward for meeting a challenge is sweeter than that of floating effortlessly toward a bar set too low.

There are some tools and tricks that can help you keep the motivated momentum, such as checklists and milestones—giving yourself personal rewards for reaching them is also a help. This could be daily, even: for every X amount of time spent working toward your goal, you earn X reward. These little payoffs are psychological tricks to keep you working toward your ultimate goal. Another motivator to keep you setting goals and achieving them is to set more goals. As in the opening quotation, once one summit is reached, there is yet another out there to climb. Setting goals eventually becomes a life-long habit, one that reaps positive rewards in a continuous loop. Finally, if you have started to lose motivation for the extra side hustle you may have taken up; this section ends with some ideas for other kinds of additional challenges for those who wish to keep upping the ante for their lifestyle and financial goals.

CHAPTER 10:
Actionable Tasks: Checklists, Milestones, and Sustainability

A goal is supposed to define where you are going, long term, while a milestone is a signpost that lets you know that you are on your way. Think of the analogy when taking a driving trip across the country: your goal is to reach Los Angeles, and each mile marker along with the freeway lets you know how far you've come. Checklists are visual representations of how to chart your progress: Milestone 1 requires these three actions, and then as you do them, you check each one off, eventually hitting another milestone toward your ultimate goal. As previously discussed, one of the most important parts of setting goals—especially big ones, like financial security or career success—is breaking them down into manageable parts. Without action, you lose momentum, so the best way to ensure that you will eventually reach your destination is to set up a daily checklist of actionable tasks that you can add up into milestones and, finally, achievable goals. For example, if you're saving for retirement, a daily task might be to take your lunch to work rather than eat out, while a monthly task would be to put away ten to fifteen percent of your income into savings or a retirement account. A milestone would be when you've managed to save X amount of dollars toward the ultimate goal of XXX amount of dollars.

This logic doesn't just work for the big long-term goals like saving for retirement or trying to build a start-up company. These ideas can be put to good use in your daily habits and routine in order to help you become a more productive and ultimately more successful person. This is as much about changing your mindset through actionable tasks as it is about meeting specific goals.

There are a few simple things that you can incorporate into your life that will keep you fresh, productive, and motivated. First, wake up a little earlier: the most successful CEOs in the country all routinely report that they get up before 6:00 a.m. Now, this does not mean depriving yourself of sleep, of course; it means that the old cliché "the early bird gets the worm" may not be far off the truth. Second, take a quick jog with that extra time you have in the morning. Most studies show that light running is the best way to jump-starts your brain—better than excessive doses of caffeine. Third, become more mindful and engaged with colleagues and others: send a thank you note to a team member or a client who has been valuable; take the time to have a meaningful discussion with someone at work; become involved with an online community (mastermind groups, potentially, as discussed in Chapter 9). All of these habits have the effect of building your reputation as an engaged and thoughtful person, engendering goodwill, as well as increasing your network of support and inspiration. Last, don't just organize your calendar or journal: organize your home and office. Time spent looking for missing items or shuffling through papers to get to the right one is time wasted, especially if it happens on a daily basis. The well-organized mind has little to fear.

While all of the above may not seem directly related to setting goals and keeping them, they are indeed the core of the many little good habits that you can develop which will eventually turn you into a natural seeker and keeper of goals. Motivation is as much about maintaining order and a semblance of control over your personal and professional life as it is about setting specific and realistic goals.

The other psychological factor here is that, while we all love a challenge, we only love it up to a point. The fact of the matter is that the "burn out" zone appears on either side of the spectrum: if you play golf with a three-year-old toddler, you'll quickly get bored (or frustrated); likewise, if you play golf against Tiger Woods, you'll quickly get overwhelmed (and frustrated). There is what James Clear, in his book *Atomic Habits*, calls the Goldilocks Rule: if you play golf with someone of equal talent and experience, then the challenge is rewarding and even fun. Not too hot, not too cold, but just right (astrophysicists also refer to a "Goldilocks Zone" with regard to finding a planet out in the universe that might be habitable like earth). We reach our peak motivation when facing a challenge that is not too difficult, not too easy but pushes us to—not beyond—the limits of our abilities.

Educational theorist Mike Rose, in his book *Lives on the Boundary*, uses the same sort of analogy to describe student success. He wrote, "Students float to the mark you set." If you set the mark too low, then students will just bump their head on the ceiling and stay working at sub-par levels. If you set the mark high, students will reach up to meet it. But if you set the mark unmanageably high, students will get frustrated and deflate. This is the kind of thinking we need to do for ourselves when setting goals: they need to be challenging enough that we stretch our abilities, thus keeping us interested and motivated, but not so challenging that we end up getting frustrated and giving up.

Another point made by Clear is that to stay motivated, we must measure our progress and find ways to receive immediate feedback. He uses the example of the comedian, actor, and writer Steve Martin, who struggled for many years to find success before his ultimate breakthrough. One of the things that kept him motivated was to hear the immediate laughter after telling a joke: this was a measure in the immediate moment of success. Likewise, an athlete gets immediate feedback when he or she wins a tournament; within training, that typically comes from a coach. The challenge for the rest of us in staying motivated is to find ways to garner feedback—keeping checklists and marking milestones is one way to stay self-motivated and on track for long-term success.

CHAPTER 11:
Finding Your Future: Goals Beyond the Now

Besides the daily accountability, another factor that keeps us motivated to achieve our goals is contemplating the future—not just in an abstract way, but in a way that encourages you to envision your life as you would like it to be in ten or twenty years' time. The daily checklists and marking of milestones will keep you doing what you need to in order to accomplish that reality, but the psychological nature of believing in yourself and pushing hard for what you want cannot be understated. Setting big goals is part of the motivation to push hard to get them done. Besides vision boards and the like, there are other things that can help keep your present actively focused on what you want your future to be.

The following technique has been used by successful people for many years (*CBS This Morning* actually has a segment that is similar to this idea): write a letter to your future self. Envision yourself at 75 or 80 and write a letter about all you have accomplished, about all the hard work it took to get there, about how proud you are of your full and successful life. Tuck it away somewhere and read it on occasion. This motivates you to make that hopeful letter a real success.

Ask yourself five probing "why" questions: why do I want to achieve this goal? Why am I working so hard? Why do I want more money? Why do I want a family? Why do I want long-term security? Whatever best fits your situation. These questions require you to do some soul searching, as it were, to figure out what your underlying motivations are and to recalibrate, if need be, to refocus on the long game.

Think about immediate motivators: what motivates you to act in real-time, to tackle actionable tasks? This can be a rewarding scenario. For example, if one of your goals is to lose weight, then put your treadmill in front of the television so you cannot watch your favorite shows without doing some walking: effort and payoff. Back in the days of video stores, it was easy to make yourself walk to the store to obtain your video and back; this was the price to pay for lounging on the couch for two hours. Or, if you want to excel at freelance work—let's use writing as an example—set yourself a reward of ice cream or take-out for every ten thousand words you write. If you have small rewards along the way, then the effort becomes easier, even more enjoyable.

Don't forget about your vision board, and don't neglect its contents, either. As you work through your daily checklists and reach milestones, your original vision may shift—it may grow larger, more expansive—so add to your vision board as you go, creating new visual cues that help you to maintain the motivation that started you on this journey in the first place.

Think about the long-term goals you have set. Often, in the short term, we are really just fighting fires, solving problems as they arise and dealing with our busy lives at every juncture. But keeping the bigger picture in mind helps us to strike a balance between everyday problem solving and executing actionable tasks that lead to future actualization of larger goals. Basically, don't get bogged down in the everyday all the time. Take time out each day to contemplate and to take action on something for your future success.

If you find yourself really struggling with motivation, especially if you are feeling overwhelmed by all that you have to accomplish on a daily basis, take a second. Hit the pause button. Spend some time reflecting on your goals and prioritize, if need be. If the first pitfall that most people make in setting goals is making them overly abstract without a clear action plan, then the second most common pitfall is taking on too many goals. Settle on two or three for the future, with one of them always being something about your personal well-being. This is another factor to consider carefully: if you are not taking care of yourself, then there is little chance that you can take care of anyone or anything else. A personal wellness goal, along with one or two other life goals—a career ambition, a retirement plan—is about all that one can focus on at a time. Certainly, we all have many, many worthy goals; it is simply about making smart and healthy decisions about what is best and right for you in the short term and the long.

With regard to the above, it also helps to look at your situation from two points of view: as discussed above, looking toward an imagined future is one sure why of psychologically pumping yourself up, and it can help. But when you start to feel overwhelmed, prioritizing your goals can help, as well as taking some time to review your situation objectively. Goals should be specific and attainable—and you *should* dream big—but it doesn't mean that you should never re-evaluate. So your side business hasn't taken off the way you expected; take a second to review why that might be, see if you can regroup to fix it, or simply adjust your goal—perhaps this isn't the right business for you, at least at this time. This doesn't mean abandoning goals, and it certainly doesn't mean that you have failed; it simply means that logically speaking, this isn't working right now. Figure out why and work to adjust it.

Maintaining motivation isn't always easy or simple, nor should it be. As Socrates allegedly said, "the unexamined life is not worth living." We should all take a step back and remember what we are working for and why we are working so hard for it. Examining where you are and envisioning where you want to be are powerful motivators for future success and happiness.

CHAPTER 12:
More Side Hustles for All Types

One of the ways in which you might recalibrate, should you be losing motivation, is to think on different projects that might propel you to your original goal. As discussed earlier, side hustles are an excellent way to earn a bit of extra cash, pursue a passion, or develop an entrepreneurial side gig that could end up a fruitful success. In Chapter 6, there were a few general ideas on what to look for in a side hustle. Here are some more ideas for other projects, should you be looking to expand or regroup. There are opportunities for charismatic types, for creative types, for analytical types, and for nurturing types. See below for some ideas of side hustles—some obvious and very visible, some more adventurous and obscure—available today.

- Driving for a service: of course, Uber and Lyft are ubiquitous these days, and as established companies, they are an easy bet for some quick cash without much effort other than time.
- In addition to the general driving offered by some companies, there are now

specialized services such as Door Dash and UberEATS that specialize in food deliveries.
- Become a notary public: for fees of around $100, you can become a notary public and sell your services for whatever fee you wish (as long as the market can bear it). Some people specialize in particular kinds of notary work, such as mortgage signings—this creates a unique clientele that will always be in demand, should you have the marketing skills to get your name out there.
- Provide feedback on new products for companies via customer interviews. There are sites out there (such as Respondent) that allow you to do this remotely, as per piece paid work.
- There are also online surveys through sites such as Survey Junkie and Swagbucks that pay you to fill out surveys. This won't net a lot of money, of course, but can provide a few extra dollars here and there. Be sure to read terms carefully—some sites require a certain amount of surveys done before they will pay.
- Teach English online: there are numerous companies out there who offer hourly pay for teaching English to non-native

speakers. Typically, this requires video interface and, often, you have to deal with time zones. Nevertheless, this is not only a good way to make some extra money but a fulfilling project, as well.

- There are also educational sites that want online tutors. If you are good in a specific subject—especially math or English—then there are many opportunities out there, though most require higher education qualifications.
- There are even sites wherein you can teach online. If you are qualified and certified, of course, there are specific schools that offer online courses. However, there are also sites such as Udemy wherein you create your own course to teach on something you have expertise in. On Udemy, you set your own tuition rate.
- In all of our digitally focused ideas, we often forget about some very dependable, old-fashioned ones: catering is another way to capitalize on a skill set to make some extra money. This can take any form you want, really, from baking cookies for corporate meetings to party planning to innovative in-home dining. Marketing yourself is key if you wish to grow your business.

- TaskRabbit is an application most people have heard of. Sign on to execute tasks for others to make extra money.
- Not only does the internet age demand freelance writers, but there are also opportunities for editors and proofreaders, as well—and to think, I've spent most of my working life proofreading other peoples' work for free!
- Don't dismiss self-publishing, either. If you can write a decent book on an interesting topic and sell it on Kindle, then you can earn royalties in perpetuity. Most self-publishing has significant costs upfront, but if you are skilled in marketing your work, you will recoup your investment and then some.
- Some of these have already been mentioned, but there is a whole world of opportunities out there for selling your goods and services: Etsy, of course, is famous for its unique, handmade crafts, but there is also Fiverr, wherein you sell services for around $5 a pop, and Teespring where you can sell your own t-shirt designs.
- Podcasts have exploded in recent years, so competition keeps getting tougher. However, with a unique idea and a

singular voice, you can make significant money through sponsorships. It does require some equipment upfront, but it can be a very lucrative prospect.
- Household skills are also valuable in the gig economy: knife sharpening is an arena in which some have had success (and the clientele is built-on repeat customers), and doing alterations, general sewing, or laundry services have been around since long before the digital age. Certainly, childcare and pet walkers have been able to capitalize on the side hustle for ages. The personal chef market has also expanded in recent years, so if you're a solid cook with some good marketing skills, you can put that to work, as well.
- Going outside the interior of the household, car-washing and detailing are ways to make the most financial sense of your weekends. If you're handy with tools, the demand for unique hand-crafted furniture shows no signs of letting up.
- If you're talented with technology, your services could be in high demand, from troubleshooting computers (think GeekSquad) to designing web sites to making marketing banners and so on.

- Real estate has always offered a number of opportunities, from real estate agents to appraisers to home inspectors. All of these requiring licensing, but they offer a good return on the investment should you wish to devote enough time to it.
- Shopping services are also on the rise, from the old school mystery shopper to the personal shopper to the employee filling grocery orders for a pick-up. These can be fun and simple ways to bulk up your bank account.

There are many more side hustles—some that have yet to be thought of—that can allow you to develop a skill, capitalize on the one you already have, or otherwise make some extra money to invest for short-term gain or long-term financial security. These examples motivate us to think beyond business as usual and see what might spark the next great idea.

PART V:
Inspiring Examples

"What you get by achieving your goals is not as important as what you become by achieving your goals."

– *Henry David Thoreau*

What is entrepreneurship? It is a spirit and a strategy, a dream and a determination. Entrepreneurs take the road less traveled; they encounter pitfalls and roadblocks, obstacles of all sorts, but they keep to it because they believe in their goals, and they have a plan to stick to them no matter what may come. Entrepreneurs have several common characteristics: a desire for autonomy, to be your own boss; a sense of purpose with a very clear vision for the future; a flexibility that allows them to roll with the punches, as it was, and regroup; and eventually all of the previous leads to financial success and a lasting legacy. The best entrepreneurs don't just leave behind companies; they leave behind lasting marks on the cultural sphere, whether through radical technological innovation or philanthropic engagement—or both.

If you decide that part of your goal setting strategy is to put into place some entrepreneurial thinking, there is no better place to look than some of the most inspiring examples of creative thinkers who have set goals, stuck to them, and reaped enormous success as a result. Certainly, these paths aren't easy or simple, and it takes hard work, determination, and innovative ideas to realize your biggest dreams. But realize them you can, by following all of the tips and techniques outlined throughout this book, and following your own desires and dreams.

When we think of famous entrepreneurs, many names pop up immediately: tech giants like Bill Gates and Mark Zuckerberg, trailblazers like Richard Branson, savvy investors like Warren Buffet, or media moguls like Oprah Winfrey. These people all come from vastly different backgrounds and have built their empires on vastly different products and ideas. What they all have in common is a desire to set goals and a determination to reach them. Innovative ideas, intelligent business strategies, and limitless boundaries all have helped these people reach the pinnacle of their professions. Reviewing their career choices and struggles can certainly be inspiring to those of us just starting out.

Yet, it is not only the famous and the fabulously wealthy that can inspire us on our road to greatness. It is also the up and coming crop of entrepreneurs who are taking advantage of the new changes being wrought on our economy. These people are able to use new technology and new ways of doing business in order to begin to build their own empires. Turning a so-called side hustle into a prosperous business is no small feat. In the following chapter, you will hear a few of their stories, and then in the next, some advice and stories from famous entrepreneurs to inspire you to continue on your journey of setting goals and reaching for the sky.

CHAPTER 13:
Budding Entrepreneurs: Side Hustle Success Stories

Here are examples of some truly remarkable people, who actually look and seem a lot like you or me. These are people who had solid day jobs, a decent income, and a bit of stability—but they wanted more and had an idea. They all started side hustle businesses, managing to turn them into successful independent ventures. They are an inspiration to all of us who have a dream, whether it be creative or financial or both, and are striving to achieve it. Acknowledgments to The Balance for first bringing light to their stories.

Miss Design Berry: Kristin Berry

As a young woman, Ms. Berry moved to New York City—one of the most expensive cities in the world, as we know—and worked a full-time job in advertising for the pharmaceutical industry. She quickly realized that, while her job was rewarding and secure, she still needed some extra money to make ends meet comfortably. Thus, she did what a lot of creative people do: she opened up an Etsy shop selling her designs, logos, and illustrations. Keeping careful track of her progress, Ms. Berry noticed that one of her niches was performing better than any of the others: her wedding designs.

Thus, she focused her energies on that part of the business, and within two years, hired her first employee. Shortly thereafter, she was able to leave her day job and launched MissDesignBerry.com in 2015. From one employee to twenty employees who work remotely for her, Ms. Berry is able to work from home, overseeing her growing business. Revenue was at nearly a million dollars as of May of 2019.

Her advice is simple: if you have an idea, then just get started. "There is no perfect time, perfect product or perfect idea," she says. And there is no time like the present to take a gamble with your own. She cautions, however, to keep up with your day job until you are certain that your efforts will create a lucrative return. Be consistent and persistent, and this kind of success can be yours.

Philosophie Group, Inc.: Skot Carruth

Mr. Carruth began his professional life with a very promising and potentially lucrative career, that of an investment banker. However, with the financial crisis of 2008, his once secure career in banking came to an abrupt end. He found himself working, albeit not happily, as an accountant and began to consider other career paths.

Stuck in what he felt was a dead-end job, Mr. Carruth began designing web sites on the side, something that he had dabbled with since a young teenager. Carefully investing funds that he garnered from his accounting job, he launched an innovative design firm, Philosophie Group, Inc.

With a partner, Mr. Carruth has built the company into a nearly eight-figure earner with 40 employees across three offices. His advice is to leverage the money that you earn from your steady full-time job into your side hustle—if it's something you're truly passionate about and confident in. Keeping the "safety net" of your day job "forces you to spend your time wisely, and removes the financial stress that may cause you to make bad decisions."

Impressa Solutions: Julie T. Ewald

An adventurous traveler, Ms. Ewald was living abroad in Italy when she finally ran out of money. She tried her hand at freelance writing but found that it wasn't really enough to keep her afloat. Still, she knew she had a marketable skillset, so she signed up for UpWork after moving back to the United States. Within a couple of days, all of her bids were accepted, and she was on her way to start of a new career.

In order to capitalize on her early success, Ms. Ewald spends time developing her skills, turning her attention not only to the craft of writing but also to the demands of marketing. As she puts it, "I continued to hone my skills and learn more about digital marketing, as my writing was being used for articles, blog posts, and website content for various businesses and brands."

At this point, she became so busy that she started having to turn clients away; it was time to branch out on her own. Thus, Impressa Solutions was born, an inbound marketing agency with several employees. Her freelance side hustle had morphed into a fully-fledged business within ten months. Ms. Ewald now offers her advice to others via coaching on how to get started in the online space.

The Amani Experience: Amani Roberts

Working in corporate America did little to fulfill the dreams of Mr. Roberts, so he decided to pursue his passion: DJing as a side hustle.

Keeping his day job, Mr. Roberts worked nights and weekends as a DJ to build up a reputation and a clientele base.

A few years later, Mr. Roberts realized that he had the makings of security and success with his Djing side hustle. "I realized it was time to go full time when the revenue I was earning was half of my current salary. This gave me a good foundation to build upon while going full-time," he says.

Four years into his experiment, he started The Amani Experience, a self-owned DJ company. His advice to others is to diversify: Mr. Roberts doesn't earn all his money simply from DJing; rather, he also creates original music for commercial venues (advertising, videos), as well as teaches lessons in DJing itself. Finally, he says that the journey is not easy—there will be bumps along the road. Perseverance is key, he says, as it "will make the journey worthwhile."

Pet Sitter: Melanie Lewis

While it may seem inconceivable, making a living as a pet sitter is exactly what Ms. Lewis was able to do. She was working as a freelance writer when a friend suggested she check out pet sitting on the site Rover.com to earn some extra money. Ms. Lewis already had two dogs, so she was familiar with the challenges of keeping and caring for pets. Still, in the arena of pet sitting, there is lots of competition, so Ms. Lewis knew that she would have to do something different in order to really stand out and be successful.

Instead of marketing herself as a traditional kennel-style room and board experience, she offered her clients a "home away from home" experience for their beloved pets. Rather than an ascetic stay in a stiffly professional facility, this would be a romp through the park and lots of love at home.

The response was nearly instantaneous, she says. "I was always fully booked, and I started booking new client stays up to four to six weeks out. I decided to become a full-time pet sitter when I was able to hit my max capacity of dogs every day." That goal turned into a tangible reality early in 2016.

Her main advice is to gauge your commitment carefully, to be sure that you have the stamina to take on a start-up business. There is the work itself, but also the marketing and the potential financial instability while the business gets up and running. She says that financial security is the most important: without it, you will likely end up back in a typical day job. "The question to ask yourself before you make the switch to full-time is whether or not you have the capacity—time, energy, enthusiasm—and financial stability to do so," she says.

All of the above entrepreneurs are young, energetic, goal-orientated people who turned a side hustle into a golden opportunity for personal fulfillment and financial success. What they have achieved, through a combination of creativity and determination is well within the grasp of anyone who has an interesting idea and a solid plan.

CHAPTER 14:
Famous Entrepreneurs: Advice from Above

While it takes a desire for autonomy, a clear sense of purpose and an ability to be flexible, entrepreneurship is within the reach of anyone who wishes to strive for it—as long as they have a good plan and firm footing. There are numerous examples of very famous, very wealthy, and often philanthropic entrepreneurs out there still working today. If you are thinking about embarking on this difficult but ultimately satisfying journey, some advice from those well-established figures that have come before you is certainly well taken.

Bill Gates is one of the most recognizable figures in the world, founder of the Microsoft Empire and now co-curator of the Bill and Melinda Gates Foundation, dedicated to human rights philanthropy throughout the world. Obviously, an enormously successful billionaire, Gates has in recent years come across as a humble and humanitarian businessman. He once said, "It's fine to celebrate success but it is more important to heed the lessons of failure," which is a quotation that any aspiring entrepreneur would do well to abide by. One of the fascinating early stories about Microsoft's success and Gates's rise to fame and fortune is when he actually worked on the call center floor. This was back in 1989 when Microsoft wasn't quite the household name it is today, but it was still a multi-million dollar business with offices and support centers throughout the country. While taking a look around one of these facilities, Gates asked if he could take a tech support call. Calling himself William, he answered the call, patiently listened to the client, walked them through the problem, and gave them a solution. The customer was so pleased that when he called back, he asked for William by name. The lesson in this is that, no matter how important we may seem or how famous we may be, it is crucial not to lose sight of the nuts and bolts of your business. This is significant not only for simple oversight but also for fostering a culture of humble success: keep your eye on the prize via each interaction of the day.

Mark Zuckerberg became an extraordinarily successful and an extraordinarily wealthy individual at a very early age. Despite the recent reservations regarding Facebook and privacy, it is still the largest and most used social networking site in the world. Some lessons that other budding entrepreneurs could learn from the arc of Zuckerberg's career are both simple and bold. For starters, take up something about which you are passionate: without the passion, it can be hard to hold on during the rough times. Zuckerberg is also a fan of thinking big—as anyone in this chapter is—but he emphasizes starting small. Implementing a grand vision one step at a time is a steady way to overall success. He also sounds a note of caution when moving forward with new ideas, following the notion that you should explore thoroughly before you commit absolutely; it's best to be aware of potential pitfalls before it's too late to remedy them. Like many famous entrepreneurs, Zuckerberg has often heralded the mantra to hire the right people; if you surround yourself with talent and creativity, the combined combustion leads to brilliant and original ideas. He is also a lifelong learner, committed to always working to making the product better—lately, he's under pressure to continue that trend—and expanding as you go.

Richard Branson, explorer and founder of Virgin Records, Virgin Airlines, and Virgin Galactic (along with other ventures), has some simple rules to follow if you want to be a successful entrepreneur. First and foremost, money is not the key to success, according to

Branson. If you measure your success simply by how much money you make, then you are missing the point of entrepreneurship: continually setting goals to make the world a better place. Second, he also recommends that you conduct business face-to-face as often as you can; the personal touch is imperative to establishing trustworthy networks. Branson also puts an emphasis on the fun: if you're not having fun doing it, it's not worth doing is his motto. Get outside as often as you can, and enjoy the wonders of the natural world. He doesn't believe in doing things by half measures, either; dream big and be fearless is his advice because that's the only way to achieve great things. Branson also proffers the advice that you should learn as you go; be nimble and flexible, and every obstacle will begin to look like an opportunity.

Warren Buffet is a regular guy with a homespun personality who just happens to be one of the most brilliant investors of all time. He amassed a fortune through shrewd deals and innovative thinking. While his number one piece of advice is a bit tongue in cheek—"never lose money"—it essentially calls our attention to the fact that operating at a loss is always more difficult than the contrary. Basically, carefully think through your decisions, and avoid unnecessarily risky ones. He's also a fan of value, especially when it comes to investing. He also gives every sound advice to avoid debt, especially any debt with high-interest rates; this is a vicious cycle from which it is difficult to emerge. Last, not only should you invest in yourself, but you should also wholeheartedly invest in others through philanthropy. He, along with Bill and Melinda Gates and others have taken the Giving Pledge, promising to give away the bulk of his wealth to charitable causes upon his death.

Oprah Winfrey is an undoubtedly endless found of wisdom and goodwill. She is one of the rare billionaires who still feel as friendly and reassuring as your next-door neighbor. Her inspiration has touched people for decades, and she as some very pragmatic, tangible advice for those wanting to start out in business, as well. First, she reminds us that success takes time; for the vast majority of us, overnight success is an urban legend. Be patient and you will eventually persevere. Second, she is also unabashedly in favor of self-promotion, which often gets a bad rap. There is nothing wrong with using yourself to expand and support your brand (*O Magazine*, *OWN* network, and so on). Surrounding yourself with talented people is another hallmark of the Oprah brand; from Dr. Phil to Nate Berkus, Oprah has utilized talented people to expand her own reach, as well as to launch the careers of others. Oprah also recognizes that value of negotiating good deals; rather than capitalizing on her early success by merely renegotiating a higher salary, she instead parlayed that into the ownership of the company itself. In this way, she created more leverage and more control over her own brand. Last, one simply cannot think of Oprah without also thinking of her famous generosity: you have to give well to get well could be her unofficial motto. Not only does it draw attention to your brand (giving cars away is excellent free advertising), but it also generates good karma for you and the people who care about your brand.

CHAPTER 15:
Goal Setting for Success

All of the advice, tips, and techniques outlined throughout this book can be boiled down to one simple thing: setting goals is key to future success. Even if you're busy, even if you're pulled in many different directions at once, you must take the time and effort toward developing your own personal and professional goals. Without taking the time to focus on yourself, you lose sight of how to take care of everyone else. The prime example of that is in maintaining your health: if you aren't well, then how can you make sure that others are well, too? Thus, setting your own goals empowers you to build a secure future and, ultimately, to care for others in the process.

While we have covered the following ideas in detail at different points throughout the book, it is imperative to have a final reminder of what the overall destination is. Setting goals is not a purely scientific process—it requires a fair amount of moxie and psychological motivation, not to mention an emotional passion for what you desire—but it does follow some fairly basic rules that apply to any endeavor you wish to undertake.

First, set goals that motivate you. This is more difficult sometimes than it sounds, depending on the goal. For one small example, say you wish to lose weight—an admirable goal for anyone who wants to improve his or her health—however it is often much easier said than done. In this example, it's not so much the end result of the goal itself that will motivate you—lost weight, healthier you—but the reasons why you'd like to achieve that goal. Creating a healthier you is quite abstract and hard to imagine while you are sweating on the treadmill or hitting the snooze button early in the morning; thus, it helps to have more concrete goals, as well. Think of this in terms of the short term versus the long term: the short term goal is to lose weight so that you can fit into a dress or a suit for a special occasion, or get fitter for your upcoming vacation plans. These are goals that have a built-in time frame, as well as a specific motivation. Now, ultimately, that won't be enough to keep you motivated past the special occasion or vacation; that's where the long term comes in. You must be motivated beyond the present instant fulfillment to keep the weight loss going or to keep the weight off. The long-term goal is the healthier you, and once you achieve the short term part of it; it becomes easier to realize the long-term aspiration. Once you have lost weight and feel fitter, healthier, it becomes easier to envision that as a lifestyle change rather than a momentary goal.

Second, use SMART goals for the best results. The best way to attain your goals is to follow the SMART goal formula, an acronym for Specific, Measurable, Achievable, Relevant, and Time-Bound. Using the example above, setting the goal to "lose weight" isn't enough. Setting a specific goal to lose 35 pounds, which has the built-in attribute of being measurable? It is clearly achievable, based on the assumption that this particular number would not put you dangerously underweight, of course. The relevance comes in answering the "whys" from above: why am I doing this? Firstly, because I want to look good for a particular occasion; secondly, because I want to be happier with myself and feel healthier. Bind yourself to a reasonable time frame; don't let the time-bound rule trip up the achievable one by setting unreasonable demands on yourself. Losing 35 pounds over six months or a year is a reasonable amount of time that won't set you up for failure.

Third, put your goals into writing, a concrete reminder of where you want to go. When goals remain lofty ideas, then they rarely are reached.

This goes for everything from the personal goal as discussed above—weight loss—to the more complicated goals such as saving money for retirement or starting a business. It seems to go without saying that when starting a business or building for retirement, you would want to write things down, keep a checklist, and establish plans and milestones. But this is also important for the seemingly smaller personal goals, as well. If you wish to lose weight, but never write it down or track your progress, then it will remain an elusive goal at best. Throughout the book, there are suggestions on how to hold yourself accountable for any goal you are trying to reach, from using vision boards to joining mastermind groups.

Fourth, create a clear action plan. Again, establish a goal is one step, but actualizing it is a whole series of other steps. It doesn't matter whether the goal is personal, professional, or financial, if you do not have a clear plan of what you intend to do to get there than it is nearly impossible to achieve. As discussed above, this requires executing tasks in the short term—today, this week, next month—as well as establishing parameters for an endpoint—ten years from now, whatever the case may be. Keeping track of your actions is also crucial, and there are several techniques that can assist you there, from applications on your phone to online programs to old-fashioned journaling and so on. Maintaining motivation is easier when you can visually remind yourself of the progress that you have thus far made. It's a lot harder to give up on something when you've come so far.

Fifth, stick to the plan with a clear-eyed vision of your long-term goal(s). The last bit of advice here is often the toughest to follow. Life happens, all around us, every moment of every day. We do not often have the luxury to determine what to prioritize all the time. We have obligations to people and organizations other than ourselves. Still, that is the beauty of creating a clear and well-thought-out plan: even when we are distracted by the little things, we can commit to a goal that we have written down, have created a clear action plan for, and feel passionate about. Straying off the track for one day or even one month can be overcome with a recommitment to what you want for your life in the long run. Give this book a re-read for some reinforcement.

Conclusion

As we all know, we all live busy, productive, sometimes hectic lives: work, school, family, and friends often take precedence over our own personal aspirations. Occasionally, it feels that we are simply running in place, just trying to keep up with what we already have on our plates. Unfortunately, the larger goals we have in mind—for creative success, for financial security—often fall by the wayside. Having an action plan to set goals, maintain momentum, and stay motivated to keep meeting milestones is the only sure way to achieve what you deserve. Following the tips and techniques proffered throughout this book should give you a firm footing on how to get started, along with some inspirational assistance to boot.

Once you have established your parameters and worked towards securing your financial and personal goals, keep preparing for the future and stay focused on maintaining your momentum. This requires setting realistic goals and developing an action plan that is manageable and specific. Keep track with strong organization, checklists, milestones and/or mastermind groups. The pathway to success is winding, for certain, but with some carefully considered actions and follow-through, you are sure to get where you want to go.

Heed the advice and examples of the great entrepreneurs, and develop your dreams into concrete ideas and financial success. Busy people can still take advantage of everything that life has to offer—balancing your personal life with your professional aspirations, creating your own individual success story—with some astute planning and determined preparation. Here's to your continuing success, from one goal to the next!

www.ingramcontent.com/pod-product-compliance
Lightning Source LLC
Chambersburg PA
CBHW070421220526
45466CB00004B/1494